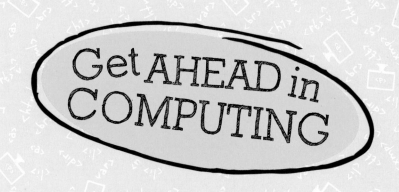

Get AHEAD in COMPUTING

WEBPAGE Design

Clive Gifford

WAYLAND

Wayland
Carmelite House
50 Victoria Embankment
London EC4Y 0DZ

Wayland Australia
Level 17/207 Kent Street
Sydney, NSW 2000

Produced for Wayland by
White-Thomson Publishing Ltd
www.wtpub.co.uk
01273 479982

Project Editor: Sonya Newland
Designer: Rocket Design (East Anglia) Ltd

A catalogue record for this title is available
from the British Library.

ISBN: 978 1 5263 0406 3

Printed in China

Wayland, part of Hachette Children's Group
and published by Hodder and Stoughton Limited

www.hachette.co.uk

Disclaimer: The website addresses (URLs) included in this book were valid at the
time of going to press. However, because of the nature of the Internet, it is possible
that some addresses may have changed, or sites may have changed or closed down
since publication. While the author and publisher regret any inconvenience this may
cause the readers, no responsibility for any such changes can be accepted by either
the author or the publisher.

Note to readers: Words highlighted in bold appear in the Glossary on page 30.

Contents

Welcome to the World Wide Web

From humble beginnings, running on a single computer, the **World Wide Web** (www) has become the world's biggest source of information and entertainment. Every day, hundreds of millions of people look at pages of images, text and videos found on the World Wide Web.

What is the Web?

Some people think that the **Internet** and the World Wide Web are the same thing. They are not:

• The Internet is the name given to the giant system of computer networks that spans the world. It connects millions of computers, allowing them to send digital data such as emails or files to one another.

• The World Wide Web is a collection of information that can be accessed using the Internet. The Web consists of millions of websites containing documents, links and files. These can be viewed by almost any device that can access the Internet.

People use smartphones, tablets and smart TVs, as well as computers, to enjoy websites.

People were slow at first to catch on to the World Wide Web. In 1993, there were just 130 websites around the world. Numbers quickly rose, however. By 2000, there were 17 million websites. Seventeen years later, there are over one billion!

Websites vary greatly. Some are simple, single-page adverts or personal pages created by individuals. Others are built by companies or governments. Some websites are vast, containing thousands of different pages. By 2017, the English language version of Wikipedia – the encyclopaedia website – contained over 5.3 million pages!

COMPUTER Hero!

Tim Berners-Lee worked at a giant science centre called CERN. He was interested in finding new ways for scientists there to share information. In a flurry of activity in 1989 and 1990, and with the help of colleagues such as Robert Cailliau, Berners-Lee invented the **HTML** coding language (see page 12) to create **webpages**. He also devised the rules to transmit webpages over the Internet, known as **HTTP**. As if that wasn't enough, he also created the first webpage and **web server**, which launched on Christmas Day, 1990.

Tim Berners-Lee

TRUE STORY

What's in a Name? The World Wide Web was nearly called the Information Mesh, The Project or the Mine of Information. Berners-Lee and his colleagues considered all these names before opting for World Wide Web.

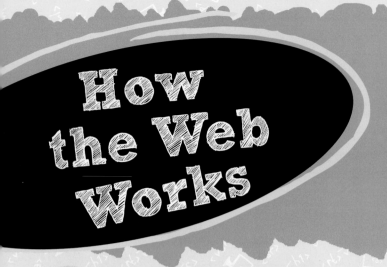

How the Web Works

When you access the World Wide Web, your simple request to see a webpage involves a number of computers and programs all working together.

 Web servers

Web servers are powerful computers that store all the files and data needed to display a website. Computers or digital devices such as smartphones and tablets that communicate with the web server are known as **clients**.

 Keeping track

Web servers keep track of which page to send to a client by using its **URL**. This is short for Uniform Resource Locator and is the address of a webpage on the World Wide Web. All webpages, and other files on the Web such as music or video files, have their own unique URL.

A user types in the address of the webpage they want to see and presses the search button.

The request travels over the Internet to the web server holding that webpage. This searches through its storage for the right files.

The server sends the page over the Internet back to the client, which displays the page on the screen.

client request

server response

web server

Understanding URLs

A URL often looks like this:

www tells the server that the file's location can be found on the World Wide Web.

http stands for the protocol (a series of rules and codes), which helps one computer talk to another.

http://www.clivelive.rocks/aboutme.html

clivelive.rocks is the domain name – the name of the website.

aboutme.html is the name of the file that is being requested. In this case it is a webpage, but it could be an image or music file.

Browsing around

The webpage is requested on the computer. When it arrives, it is displayed by a program called a web **browser** (or just browser). Popular browsers include Mozilla Firefox, Google Chrome, Safari, Internet Explorer and Opera. They all tend to have the same main buttons and features.

The **home** button will take you back to the homepage of the browser you are using.

Back and **Forward** buttons allow you to visit the webpage you were previously on and come back again.

The **refresh** button reloads the webpage. It can be used to see changes to webpages or if a page will not load.

The **address bar** is where you type in URLs or search terms to look for a website.

7

The Web Designer's Toolkit

To create websites, you need a web browser, an Internet connection, a website domain name, web hosting, and programs to write and send webpages.

Domain names

A website needs its own unique address, just like your street address, so that people can find it. This is called a domain name.

The code to the right of the dot is the top-level domain. This might be a country code such as `.au' for Australia. Alternatively it might tell you something about the website, such as .com for commercial websites or .edu for universities.

DOT WHAT?

In recent years, more top-level domains have been released including .farm, .social and even .ninja!

STRETCH YOURSELF

Name Your Site

Come up with your perfect website name. Try to keep the name short and think up alternatives. For example, if Hamsters.com is already taken, why not try Myhamsters.com or similar? Type the following address into your web browser:

 https://who.is/

You can put your website name in the box at the top and see if it is available. If it is already taken, you can see who registered the name and on what date.

Web hosting

A website needs to be stored on a web server so that it can be accessed over the Internet. This service is provided by a company called a web host. There are hundreds of web-hosting companies, and many organise packages that include the domain name and tools that make it easier to build websites.

TRUE STORY

Ker-ching Dot Com!

Some people make money by buying and selling domain names. In 2000, American computer consultant Marcelo Siero sold loans.com — a domain he got free in 1994 — for a cool US$3 million!

Uploading

A webpage is created on a web designer's computer or tablet. It is saved on that device and then **uploaded** to a web server. Most pages are sent using a set of rules called File Transfer Protocol (**FTP**).

Website writer

Websites are written in a coding language called HTML, using a text-editor program such as Notepad on a PC or TextEdit on an Apple Mac. Some people use more complex programs, such as Sublime Text or Google Web Designer, to design their web pages. These allow you to drag and drop bits of the webpage on to part of the screen and see the code that is produced.

A web designer sketches out the overall look of a webpage on a see-through screen. He is mapping out where images and text will appear before the webpage is coded.

A Selection of Sites

Before you set about building or planning your own website, it is worth looking at other websites to check out their differing designs, types and features.

Sharing sites

The world's most popular social media sites, such as Facebook, Twitter and Instagram, are all websites on the World Wide Web. They allow users to share photos, updates and other information. Other websites, like Ask A Scientist, share experts' knowledge to help you, or, like Instructables.com, give advice on repairing items.

News and sports

Hundreds of websites offer the latest news and sports results and articles. Schoolboy Tom Hadfield was just 12 when he built one of the first sports results websites back in 1995. He sold his SoccerNet website five years later to US sports broadcaster ESPN.

Online shopping

Many websites are devoted to e-commerce. This is buying and selling goods and services over the Internet, mostly via websites. It's big business. Worldwide, over US$1.9 thousand billion of goods were sold in 2016 on e-commerce websites. That's about US$6,000 for every one of the 320 million people who live in the United States!

Website warnings

Almost every subject imaginable has many websites devoted to it. The amount of choice can be confusing. In addition, many websites may not be true, up-to-date or accurate. Websites produced by major libraries, museums and respected organisations like the BBC, PBS or National Geographic are good sites to get information from.

Types of Websites

There are many different types of websites, including:

- business websites, where people can find out about companies and what they do, from local hairdressers to huge corporations

- information websites, such as Wikipedia or Encyclopedia Britannica, which contain informative articles about different topics

- directory websites, which collect website addresses and other information about related topics, such as a particular area or industry, so people know where to go for specific information

- forums, where people can communicate with one another, ask questions about certain subjects, and share information.

TRUE STORY

Mammoth Sales!
Some strange things have been sold on the auction website eBay. The first item was a broken laser pointer that sold for US$14.83 (just over £10) in 1995. Ten years later, the remains of a 50,000-year-old woolly mammoth weighing 250,000 kilograms was sold on eBay for £61,000!

STRETCH YOURSELF

Homework Helpers

Pick a science topic you're interested in, such as rockets, computer viruses or the human eye, and see what useful information you can find at these good educational websites. Note down how the websites differ in design and the ways they show information.

 www.kids.britannica.com

 www.sciencenewsforkids.org

👉 www.explainthatstuff.com

👉 www.sciencenewsforstudents.org

11

Welcome to HTML

Hyper Text Markup Language (HTML) is the language used to develop webpages. HTML's elements and **tags** do not show up on the final webpage that visitors see. Instead, these elements tell the web browser how to display the page.

 ## See the source

There are a number of ways to see the HTML behind a webpage. You can right click on a mouse while viewing a webpage, then select 'view source' or 'source' from the drop-down menu. On PCs, you can also just hold down the CTRL and U keys on your keyboard.

 ## Play tag

HTML relies on code called tags. These are angled brackets < and >. Inside the brackets is code that instructs the browser in some way. For example, <hr> means draw a horizontal line and <br> means line break.

Most other tags come in pairs – a start tag and an end tag. You can recognise an end tag as it includes a forward slash (/) just inside the first bracket.

Text tags

Lots of HTML tags act on the text of a webpage, changing it in some way. Some of the most common are shown below, along with their effects.

<u>This text is underlined</u>
This text is in bold
This text is emphasised and in italics
<centre>This text is centred</centre>

<u>This text is underlined</u>
This text is in bold
This text is emphasised and in italics
This text is centred

Heading master

Tags let you create larger text headings for parts of your page. There are six levels of headings available, from <h1> for the largest down to <h6> for the smallest.

<h1>H1 Biggest Heading</h1>
<h2>H2 Heading</h2>
<h3>H3 Heading</h3>
<h4>H4 Heading</h4>
<h5>H5 Headings getting smaller…</h5>
<h6>And H6, the smallest</h6>

H1 Biggest Heading
H2 Heading
H3 Heading
H4 Heading
H5 Headings getting smaller...
And H6, the smallest

REMEMBER!
In HTML code, all speech marks should be straight (")
not curly (" or ").

Tag-tastic

You can use more than one tag on a piece of text. So, you might want the words 'My Story' as both a heading and emphasised in italics. To do this, you could write the HTML:

<h1>My Story</h1>

COLOUR CODED

Text on an HTML page can also have its colour changed from black by using the style tag. For example:

Red is the colour
will result in: Red is the colour

The latest version of HTML includes 140 standard colours, from Peachpuff to Crimson. You can see all the named colours by typing the following into your browser:

http://www.w3schools.com/colors/colors_names.asp

13

Creating a Page

For a page to be displayed correctly by a browser, the HTML page has to follow a particular structure. HTML pages can be written in a simple text-editor program by opening a new file, typing in the code and then saving the file.

At the start

All webpages start with <!DOCTYPE html>. This lets the browser know that it is receiving an HTML document. It is followed by an <html> tag. This signals the start of the webpage. At the very bottom will be an </html> tag, ending the page.

```
<!DOCTYPE html PUBLIC "-//W3C/
<html xmlns="http://www.w3.org.
  <head>
    <meta http-equiv="Content-'
    <meta http-equiv="Content-;
    <meta http-equiv="Content-;
    <title>Document Title</tit.
    <link rev="made" href="mai.
    <link rev="start" href="./
    <style type="text/css" med
```

Header and body

Between the two header tags <head> and </head> goes the title of the webpage. The part of an HTML document that appears on the screen is found between the <body> and </body> tags. Between these two tags are all the pictures, text, tables and other parts of the page you will see.

Paragraph tag

HTML paragraphs are defined with the <p> tag and end with the </p>. Browsers automatically put a bit of space between paragraphs, so it is a good way to divide up text on a webpage.

14

Make Your First Page

Follow these steps to create your own first page and see what it looks like. Get someone to help you with any stages you are not sure about.

☞ 1 Make a new folder on your computer called 'My Webpages' or similar.

☞ 2 Open a text-editor program such as Notepad on a Windows PC. Type in the webpage html code in the panel on the right.

☞ 3 Alter the heading and the text between the <p> tags to whatever you want them to say.

☞ 4 Save the page in your new folder and give it a name ending in .html.

☞ 5 Browse the computer's files and double click quickly on your new file. A web browser program should open and display your page as it would appear on a website.

A Simple Page

```
<!DOCTYPE html>

<html>

<head>

<title>My First Webpage</title>

</head>

<body>

<h1>The heading for the page</h1>

<p>Here is where all my words will go in the first paragraph</p>

<hr>

<h3>Smaller heading</h3>

<p>Here will go the words for the second paragraph.</p>

</body>

</html>
```

TAG AFTER TAG

There are lots of HTML tags. You can view a complete list by typing the following address into your web browser:

http://www.htmldog.com/ references/html/tags/

Click on any tag and a new page will appear, describing what the tag is used for along with a real-life example in HTML code.

Adding Images

A handful of websites remain text only but most are packed with pictures, to add interest and excitement to a webpage. You can store all your website images in an 'Images' folder on your computer.

⬇ Free to use

If you want to use images from a website, you usually have to ask their permission to do so. However, some websites offer free images, including:

https://search.creativecommons.org/

http://www.freeimages.co.uk/galleries.htm

You can take your own photos or draw and scan in your own artworks.

⬇ Image tag

A single tag is all that's required to add an image in HTML. It does not need a closing tag.

webpix is the folder the image is found in.

img is an HTML tag that tells the browser that a picture of some sort will go here.

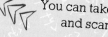
`<img src= "/webpix/picture.jpg" >`

src stands for source. It tells the browser where to go to gather the picture that is to be displayed.

picture.jpg is the name of the image file. It might be mypetdog1 or greencar, or whatever you name the file. It should always be enclosed in speech marks.

16

Your image file might be far bigger than the size you want to show it on the webpage. You can physically resize it (see below) or you can alter its height and width in the HTML code.

The image's height and width are given in number of **pixels**. These are the individual points that make up a screen. Bigger numbers mean bigger images. The numbers should always be enclosed in speech marks.

```
<img src="/images/
petdog.jpg" width="180"
height="120">
```

This image is 180 pixels wide and 120 pixels high.

```
<img src="/images/petdog.jpg"
width="90" height="60">
```

This image is half the height and width of the original.

```
<img src="/images/petdog.jpg" width="300"
height="120">
```

This image has been stretched so that it is wider than the original but just as high.

STRETCH YOURSELF

Resizing Apps
Online resizers are **apps** that allow you to resize your photos. Try one out by typing the following address into your browser:

👉 http://webresizer.com/resizer/

👉 1 Press the 'Choose file' button. Browse through your device to select an image to resize, then press the 'Upload image' button.

👉 2 Below the two pictures is a series of boxes. Enter a new number in the 'New size' box.

👉 3 Select 'Apply changes' and the resized image will appear on the page to the left. Click on the 'Download this image' button to get it back on your computer.

Why not try out the monochrome button to turn your picture black and white?

Can you add a coloured border to your image?

Jumping Around

To produce a website, you need to think about what content it will contain and how this will be organised into different, linked webpages.

Hyperlinks

To link between different parts of a website, webpages use **hyperlinks**. A text hyperlink is shown underlined and in a different colour to surrounding text. If clicked on, the link tells the browser to jump to another page or element on the World Wide Web.

WHAT SHOULD I DO NOW?

Click the link below for other titles.

See Other Great Books.

This is a list of highly recommended books to read.

COMPUTER Hero!

US academic **Ted Nelson** began Project Xanadu in 1960, to build the first easy-to-use computer network. He came up with hyperlinks to allow information to be easily accessed. His work influenced both Douglas Engelbart, who invented the computer mouse, and Tim Berners-Lee, who pioneered the World Wide Web.

Local or external

A hyperlink can instruct the browser to head to another page on the same website. This is called a local link. A link can also jump to a different website. This is called an external link.

The website address is where the browser will go. It is not displayed on the webpage.

```
<a href="https://www.hachettechildrens.co.uk/">
See Other Great Books</a>
```

This text is displayed as a hyperlink.

This tag ends the hyperlink.

Not just text

Hyperlinks do not have to be pieces of text. An image can be turned into a hyperlink.

This is the address of a gallery webpage of cat images.

This tag adds a cat image which can be clicked on, and acts as a hyperlink to go to the gallery.

```
<a href="website address/
catpix"> <img src="tabbycat.jpg"> </a>
```

STRETCH YOURSELF

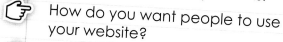

Menu matters

Hyperlinks are used in website menus to direct people around. Each menu button is an image with a hyperlink in the HTML code to jump to a different part of the site. Menus can run down one side of the page or across the top of the page, when they are called bars.

Sketch a Site Map

Plan out the perfect site map, using pens and paper. Draw a large rectangle for each webpage and write in what it will contain. Draw lines to show how the pages need to link to each other. Think about the following questions:

☞ How do you want people to use your website?

☞ Which pages do you think they will visit most?

☞ What sort of menu will you have and what will its buttons say?

☞ Where will you include hyperlinks?

19

Site, Right!

To make a great webpage, you need a good eye and smart writing as well as HTML knowledge. Try to make your pages easy to read, view and use.

Writing for the Web

Writing text for websites is a little different to writing in your diary at home or stories in class. People tend to glance at and read only parts of a webpage, so make sure what you want to say most is clearly stated. This usually means putting it near the top of the webpage.

Paragraphs should be short, and keep your writing to the point! If you refer to another page on the website, use a hyperlink rather than repeating the text. Try to use interesting headings to split up sections of text. This will help keep your visitors reading.

Making Lists

Putting text in short, neat lists can keep your webpage looking clean and uncluttered. You can make ordered lists using the <ol> tag, which will number each item, or unordered lists using the <ul> tag, which creates a bullet-point list:

```
<strong>My favourite things</strong>
<ul>
<li>My games console</li>
<li>My best friend, Steve</li>
<li>My mountain bike</li>
<li>My new pair of jeans</li>
<li>Pizza for dinner!</li>
</ul>
```

My favourite things

- My games console
- My best friend, Steve
- My mountain bike
- My new pair of jeans
- Pizza for dinner!

Dividing It Up

The <div> tag can also be useful in the design of your webpage. It can be used to split up sections of a webpage so that different styles apply to different sections. For example, you can give a section of the page a pink background by adding the following HTML code.

<div style="background-color: pink">

<h2>Pink Part of Page heading</h2>

<p>Here is a paragraph placed on a pink background</p>

<p>And here is another<p>

</div>

<p>This paragraph is not part of the pink section.</p>

TRUE STORY

Chair Man! You're never too young to become a successful website designer. Sean Kelnick was just 14 years old when he built the BizChair.com website. Six years later, it was selling US$38 million of office chairs every year!

WEBPAGE CHECKLIST

Make a habit of checking all these things before you complete a page:

- ☐ Do all your tags have a closing tag if they need one, i.e. </strong>?
- ☐ Have you put a forward slash before the tag element to close it correctly?
- ☐ Are you saving the webpage with the correct name?
- ☐ Are all your images the right size and are the files stored in the correct folders?
- ☐ If you have changed the location of the page on your website, have you altered the menu hyperlinks?

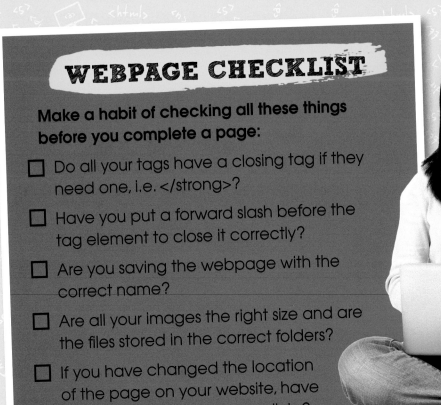

Doing It in Style

When designing a website, many web designers put all their instructions for how the webpages will look into a single document, called a **style sheet**.

What is CSS?

CSS stands for Cascading Style Sheets. It can define what colours, panels and background images are used on the webpage. CSS files can be created using a text editor in the same way as an HTML page. To apply CSS to a whole webpage, you just have to add a line of code in the header of a webpage, such as:

```
<link rel="stylesheet" type="text/css" href="stylesheetfile.css"/>
```

Style-sheet benefits

A single style sheet can be shared and used by all the webpages of a website, without the need to rewrite code for every single webpage. It helps make HTML pages less full of code so they are easier to edit.

COMPUTER Hero!

Håkon Wium Lie

Håkon Wium Lie was a young Norwegian computer programmer in the 1990s. While working with Tim Berners-Lee on the early World Wide Web, he developed the idea of CSS, which have become a web standard. Lie is now the Chief Technology Officer of web browser company Opera Software. He also owns a farm and is a politician in the Pirate Party in Norway!

Font fun

Let's look at one example of how CSS can alter the look of a webpage. Fonts are a specific design of characters that make up text. Here are some common fonts:

Arial Black

Times New Roman

Verdana

Courier New

The height and size of a font is specified in points or pixels. The bigger the number, the bigger the text.

Arial Black 8 point

Arial Black 12 point

Arial Black 16 point

Using CSS, you can alter the font, its colour and its size. Each property and value is separated from the next by a semi-colon.

Verdana

p {font-family:"Verdana"; font-size: 16pt; color: blue;}

|

Text is in blue in the Verdana font and 16 points high.

STRETCH YOURSELF

CSS in Action

To see CSS working, type the following address into your web browser:

 http://www.mezzoblue.com/zengarden/alldesigns/

Here you will see the same page of HTML code giving various makeovers with different style sheets, so the webpage looks quite different. Which is your favourite?

REMEMBER!
All words used in CSS are in American English so 'colour' is spelt 'color'.

23

Content Management Systems

Some people take the coding out of their Web work by using a one-stop website builder and a Content Management System (**CMS**).

One-stop solutions

Some companies, like Wix and Weebly, allow you to create an entire website from scratch. Users of Weebly, for example, choose a theme (the overall look) and then add different elements, such as text, photos and menu buttons, to the webpage. These can be altered in size, position and colour before the page is sent to the World Wide Web. These websites are basic CMSs, using a 'drag-and-drop' style of web design.

CMS

All the text, images and other things that go on your webpage are its content. A CMS is a clever program, or series of programs, that makes it easier to create new content and to add it to website pages without writing new HTML code.

Wordpress

People add many different CMSs to their websites, including Joomla, Squarespace and Magento. The most popular is Wordpress, which powers over a quarter of all websites that use CMSs. In 2015, one million new articles were published each day on Wordpress sites!

Many CMSs allow you to create a new paragraph of text just by typing it into a box on the screen. Once the typing is finished and the entry is sent, the CMS handles all the work needed for it to appear on a webpage. This makes it really handy for **blogs** or the news pages of websites that need new information to be displayed frequently and quickly.

TRUE STORY

Celebs on the Web! Wordpress has proven popular with new website designers, but is also used by big-name companies and celebrities. Usain Bolt and Katy Perry's official websites run using Wordpress, as does the official Angry Birds computer game website and the Official Star Wars blog!

COMPUTER Hero!

Wordpress is the most popular CMS.

In 2003, **Matt Mullenweg** and **Mike Little** began developing Wordpress as an application for people to publish blogs on the World Wide Web easily. It has since developed into a powerful Content Management System.

25

Design Over Time

The World Wide Web is not yet 30 years old, but it has undergone many changes. It has increased in size dramatically, and the websites on it have become increasingly more colourful and sophisticated.

⬇ Shrinking pics

Early websites had just a handful of pictures, which were often very small because large images slowed down the loading of the webpage. With today's fast Internet connections, most websites feature lots of colour and images, often displayed at large sizes. Some websites run background videos or **animations** at the same time.

Clive Gifford

Clive Gifford is an award-winning author of more than 60 books in both fiction and non-fiction for publishers including Hodder, Oxford University Press, Kingfisher Publications and Dorling Kindersley. He lives in Manchester, UK but travels greatly for his research and to occasionally give talks to parents, teachers and young, budding writers.

To learn more about Clive and his writing credits, please select **In Print**. For some fun and games and to learn about Clive's live visits, click on **Clive Live!**

Early webpages look tiny compared to those viewed on a large monitor today. This was partly due to the small screens on computers in the past. Websites got wider for a time, then when smartphone use boomed in the 2000s, some websites grew tall and skinny. This meant that phone users could read the site and scroll down the page.

Today, many sites are 'responsive' websites. That means they can change their shape so that they can be displayed well on smartphones, tablets, laptops and widescreen TVs.

New features

HTML itself has changed. Its latest version, HTML 5.1, was released in 2016. Each release – and the release of other apps – enables web designers to add new features to websites, from **Javascript** animations and games to social media updates.

HTML 5

STRETCH YOURSELF

Ever-Changing Websites

Websites can change greatly over time. Some may get a fresh new design or old content on their pages may be removed, altered or entire pages deleted.

You can view how some famous websites have changed their design over time by typing the following into your web browser.

 https://tinyurl.com/gqwbty4

This takes you to an article featuring some famous, long-running websites. Move the small slider bars below each website's image to see their redesigns over the years.

Added Features

As websites have developed, so web designers have sought out ways of making their webpages stand out by offering new features.

 Adding sound

Sound can be added to webpages in different ways. The HTML tag A HREF adds a hyperlink that leads a browser to a sound file. If the browser is set up properly, then it should play the file.

```
<A HREF="interview.wav">Click here to listen to Jenny speak</a>
```

This is a .wav sound file.   This text appears on the page.

 Audio controls

From HTML5 onwards, you can add new code that allows a more advanced and useful way of adding sound. It can look like the following:

Controls display a sound player on screen that allows users to play, pause and adjust the volume of the sound file.

This tag starts the audio process.

This is an mp3 sound file.

This text message is shown only if the sound file cannot be played.

```
<audio controls>
  <source src="happytune.mp3" type="audio/mpeg">
Sorry, your web browser can't play this.

</audio>
```

Web widgets

A web **widget** is a piece of reusable code that can be added to a webpage to give it an extra feature. Among the many widgets available are weather forecast panels, and simple tools including calculators that convert currencies or different measurements, such as metres into feet.

Javascript

Javascript is a programming language used to create exciting and interactive webpages. Javascript can alter the code on an HTML page, for example, to hide part of the screen or respond and display something when a button is pressed. It is often involved in making parts of a webpage move, such as a scrolling screen.

COMPUTER Hero!

The Netscape logo

Marc Andreessen was the co-author of Mosaic. This was the first widely used web browser that could display images. He went on to jointly found Netscape, which produced browsers. The company also first developed Javascript and Ning, a platform for social media.

Glossary

animation When images or models are photographed in a series of positions so they look as if they are moving when the images are shown in sequence as a film

app A small computer program, such as a game, that can be downloaded and used on mobile devices like tablets and smartphones.

blog Short for web log, a list of diary or journal entries posted on a webpage for others to read.

browser A type of program used by people to view websites on the World Wide Web.

clients Computers and other devices that 'talk' to or communicate with a web server.

CMS Short for 'Content Management System', this is a computer application that allows users to edit and alter parts of their website's content easily.

CSS Short for 'Cascading Style Sheets', this is a coding language that is used to define the style and look of a webpage.

FTP Short for 'File Transfer Protocol', this is a system that is used to transfer files from one computer to another, via a network such as the Internet.

HTML Short for 'HyperText Markup Language', this is a type of language that web pages are written in so that they can be displayed on different devices using the Internet.

HTTP Short for 'HyperText Transfer Protocol', this is a set of rules that allows computer data and files to be transferred on the World Wide Web.

hyperlink A word, phrase or image on a webpage, which when clicked on allows the user to jump to a new place in the website.

Internet A system of computer networks that connect millions of computers all over the world.

Javascript A programming language used to create interactive webpages.

pixels The dots of colour that make up an image on a screen.

style sheet A text document that gives a browser information about the design of a website.

tag A piece of code that gives direction to a browser in HTML.

upload To send a computer file from one computer to another, or if connected to a network, posting the file on the network for others to share, view and use.

URL Short for 'Uniform Resource Locator', this is a unique address for each file or webpage held on a computer network such as the Internet.

webpage A document found on the World Wide Web.

web server A computer that stores and serves up (delivers) webpages to viewers when they are connected to the Internet and they make a request.

widget Reusable code or tools that can be added to a website.

World Wide Web A collection of information that can be accessed by the Internet.

Books

The Quick Expert's Guide to Building a Website by Chris Martin (Wayland, 2012)

I'm an HTML Web Page Builder by Max Wainewright (Wayland, 2017)

Inspirational Lives: Tim Berners-Lee by Claudia Martin (Wayland, 2017)

Websites

http://www.lissaexplains.com/html.shtml
A great online tutorial about learning HTML, especially designed for kids.

http://www.yourhtmlsource.com/myfirstsite/myfirstpage.html
A handy article on creating your first webpage on a site, with lots of other tutorials on creating webpages.

https://webdesign.tutsplus.com/tutorials/web-design-for-kids-css--cms-24116
A great lesson designed for kids on how CSSs work and are used.

http://www.lissaexplains.com/javascript.shtml
A fabulous series of demos and tutorials for kids about using Javascript in websites.

http://computing.artsci.wustl.edu/help/web/resize-images-web
A useful guide to different ways of resizing images for your website.

Index

TITLES IN THE SERIES

Computing All Around Us
Input and Output
All About Algorithms
Real-World Algorithms
Sensors
Coding Decisions
In Control
Barcodes and Stock Control
Where Am I?
Money Matters
Working with Robots
3D Printing
The Internet of Things

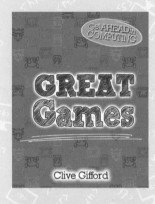

Fun on the Screen
Early Computer Games
Types of Games
Storyboards
Game Assets
Game Characters
The Game World
Game Rules and Features
Coding Games
Decision Time!
Controlling Games
Keeping Score
Testing and Launching

Keeping in Touch
Social Media History
Facebook
Instant Messaging and
    Microblogging
Sharing Snaps
Connecting to Social Media
How Information Spreads
The Business of Social Media
Signing Up and Starting Out
Keeping It Private
Smart, Safe Social Media
Social Media Issues
Cyberbullying

Welcome to the World Wide Web
How the Web Works
The Web Designer's Toolkit
A Selection of Sites
Welcome to HTML
Creating a Page
Adding Images
Jumping Around
Site, Right!
Doing It in Style
Content Management Systems
Design Over time
Added Features

Program Explosion
Operating Systems
Popular Operating Systems
Interface to Face
Data and Circuits
Files in Style
Getting Organised
It's the Business
Text Success
Words and Picture
Sounds and Music
Games, Games, Games
App Attack!

Coding your World
Algorithms in Action
Ones and Zeros
Mind your Language
Languages for Learning
Scratch!
Accurate Algorithms
Get in Step
Decisions, Decisions
Go with the Flow
Going Loopy
A Bug's Life
Coding Careers

A World of Computers
The Incredible
  Shrinking Computer
Here's the Hardware
Let's Look Inside
Data and Circuits
Memory Matters
Imput Devices
More Input Devices
Sounds Amazing
Picture Perfect
Computer Gaming
Mega and Mini Machines

Networks All Around Us
Let's Connect
The Internet
World Wide Web
Web Wonders
A World of Websites
Search Engines
Search and Filter
You've Got Mail
Social Networks
Danger Danger!
Keep It To Yourself